Keeping Track of the Money

Monthly Planner and Expense Tracker

@ Journals and Notebooks

All Rights reserved. No part of this book may be reproduced or used in any way or form or by any means whether electronic or mechanical, this means that you cannot record or photocopy any material ideas or tips that are provided in this book.

Copyright 2016

Monthly Planner and Expense Tracker

DATE DUE	EXPENSES	AMOUNT	PAID	DATE DUE	EXPENSES	AMOUNT	PAID

MONTH OF : _____
NOTES:

Goal	Achievement	Status

Monthly Planner and Expense Tracker

DATE DUE	EXPENSES	AMOUNT	PAID	DATE DUE	EXPENSES	AMOUNT	PAID

MONTH OF : _____
NOTES:

Goal	Achievement	Status

Monthly Planner and Expense Tracker

DATE DUE	EXPENSES	AMOUNT	PAID	DATE DUE	EXPENSES	AMOUNT	PAID

MONTH OF : _____
NOTES:

Goal	Achievement	Status

Monthly Planner and Expense Tracker

DATE DUE	EXPENSES	AMOUNT	PAID	DATE DUE	EXPENSES	AMOUNT	PAID

MONTH OF : _____
NOTES:

Goal	Achievement	Status

Monthly Planner and Expense Tracker

DATE DUE	EXPENSES	AMOUNT	PAID	DATE DUE	EXPENSES	AMOUNT	PAID

MONTH OF : _____
NOTES:

Goal	Achievement	Status

Monthly Planner and Expense Tracker

DATE DUE	EXPENSES	AMOUNT	PAID	DATE DUE	EXPENSES	AMOUNT	PAID

MONTH OF : _____
NOTES:

Goal	Achievement	Status

Monthly Planner and Expense Tracker

DATE DUE	EXPENSES	AMOUNT	PAID	DATE DUE	EXPENSES	AMOUNT	PAID

MONTH OF : _____
NOTES:

Goal	Achievement	Status

Monthly Planner and Expense Tracker

DATE DUE	EXPENSES	AMOUNT	PAID	DATE DUE	EXPENSES	AMOUNT	PAID

MONTH OF : _____
NOTES:

Goal	Achievement	Status

Monthly Planner and Expense Tracker

DATE DUE	EXPENSES	AMOUNT	PAID	DATE DUE	EXPENSES	AMOUNT	PAID

MONTH OF : _____
NOTES:

Goal	Achievement	Status

Monthly Planner and Expense Tracker

DATE DUE	EXPENSES	AMOUNT	PAID	DATE DUE	EXPENSES	AMOUNT	PAID

MONTH OF : _____
NOTES:

Goal	Achievement	Status

Monthly Planner and Expense Tracker

DATE DUE	EXPENSES	AMOUNT	PAID	DATE DUE	EXPENSES	AMOUNT	PAID

MONTH OF : _____
NOTES:

Goal	Achievement	Status

Monthly Planner and Expense Tracker

DATE DUE	EXPENSES	AMOUNT	PAID	DATE DUE	EXPENSES	AMOUNT	PAID

MONTH OF : _____
NOTES:

Goal	Achievement	Status

Monthly Planner and Expense Tracker

DATE DUE	EXPENSES	AMOUNT	PAID	DATE DUE	EXPENSES	AMOUNT	PAID

MONTH OF : _____
NOTES:

Goal	Achievement	Status

Monthly Planner and Expense Tracker

DATE DUE	EXPENSES	AMOUNT	PAID	DATE DUE	EXPENSES	AMOUNT	PAID

MONTH OF : _____
NOTES:

Goal	Achievement	Status

Monthly Planner and Expense Tracker

DATE DUE	EXPENSES	AMOUNT	PAID	DATE DUE	EXPENSES	AMOUNT	PAID

MONTH OF : _____
NOTES:

Goal	Achievement	Status

Monthly Planner and Expense Tracker

DATE DUE	EXPENSES	AMOUNT	PAID	DATE DUE	EXPENSES	AMOUNT	PAID

MONTH OF : _____
NOTES:

Goal	Achievement	Status

Monthly Planner and Expense Tracker

DATE DUE	EXPENSES	AMOUNT	PAID	DATE DUE	EXPENSES	AMOUNT	PAID

MONTH OF : _____
NOTES:

Goal	Achievement	Status

Monthly Planner and Expense Tracker

DATE DUE	EXPENSES	AMOUNT	PAID	DATE DUE	EXPENSES	AMOUNT	PAID

MONTH OF : _____
NOTES:

Goal	Achievement	Status

Monthly Planner and Expense Tracker

DATE DUE	EXPENSES	AMOUNT	PAID	DATE DUE	EXPENSES	AMOUNT	PAID

MONTH OF : _____

NOTES:

Goal	Achievement	Status

Monthly Planner and Expense Tracker

DATE DUE	EXPENSES	AMOUNT	PAID	DATE DUE	EXPENSES	AMOUNT	PAID

MONTH OF : _____
NOTES:

Goal	Achievement	Status

Monthly Planner and Expense Tracker

DATE DUE	EXPENSES	AMOUNT	PAID	DATE DUE	EXPENSES	AMOUNT	PAID

MONTH OF : _____
NOTES:

Goal	Achievement	Status

Monthly Planner and Expense Tracker

DATE DUE	EXPENSES	AMOUNT	PAID	DATE DUE	EXPENSES	AMOUNT	PAID

MONTH OF : _____
NOTES:

Goal	Achievement	Status

Monthly Planner and Expense Tracker

DATE DUE	EXPENSES	AMOUNT	PAID	DATE DUE	EXPENSES	AMOUNT	PAID

MONTH OF : _____
NOTES:

Goal	Achievement	Status

Monthly Planner and Expense Tracker

DATE DUE	EXPENSES	AMOUNT	PAID	DATE DUE	EXPENSES	AMOUNT	PAID

MONTH OF : _____
NOTES:

Goal	Achievement	Status

Monthly Planner and Expense Tracker

DATE DUE	EXPENSES	AMOUNT	PAID	DATE DUE	EXPENSES	AMOUNT	PAID

MONTH OF : _____
NOTES:

Goal	Achievement	Status

Monthly Planner and Expense Tracker

DATE DUE	EXPENSES	AMOUNT	PAID	DATE DUE	EXPENSES	AMOUNT	PAID

MONTH OF : _____
NOTES:

Goal	Achievement	Status

Monthly Planner and Expense Tracker

DATE DUE	EXPENSES	AMOUNT	PAID	DATE DUE	EXPENSES	AMOUNT	PAID

MONTH OF : _____
NOTES:

Goal	Achievement	Status

Monthly Planner and Expense Tracker

DATE DUE	EXPENSES	AMOUNT	PAID	DATE DUE	EXPENSES	AMOUNT	PAID

MONTH OF : _____
NOTES:

Goal	Achievement	Status

Monthly Planner and Expense Tracker

DATE DUE	EXPENSES	AMOUNT	PAID	DATE DUE	EXPENSES	AMOUNT	PAID

MONTH OF : _____
NOTES:

Goal	Achievement	Status

Monthly Planner and Expense Tracker

DATE DUE	EXPENSES	AMOUNT	PAID	DATE DUE	EXPENSES	AMOUNT	PAID

MONTH OF : _____
NOTES:

Goal	Achievement	Status

Monthly Planner and Expense Tracker

DATE DUE	EXPENSES	AMOUNT	PAID	DATE DUE	EXPENSES	AMOUNT	PAID

MONTH OF : _____
NOTES:

Goal	Achievement	Status

Monthly Planner and Expense Tracker

DATE DUE	EXPENSES	AMOUNT	PAID	DATE DUE	EXPENSES	AMOUNT	PAID

MONTH OF : _____
NOTES:

Goal	Achievement	Status

Monthly Planner and Expense Tracker

DATE DUE	EXPENSES	AMOUNT	PAID	DATE DUE	EXPENSES	AMOUNT	PAID

MONTH OF : _____
NOTES:

Goal	Achievement	Status

Monthly Planner and Expense Tracker

DATE DUE	EXPENSES	AMOUNT	PAID	DATE DUE	EXPENSES	AMOUNT	PAID

MONTH OF : _____
NOTES:

Goal	Achievement	Status

Monthly Planner and Expense Tracker

DATE DUE	EXPENSES	AMOUNT	PAID	DATE DUE	EXPENSES	AMOUNT	PAID

MONTH OF : _____
NOTES:

Goal	Achievement	Status

Monthly Planner and Expense Tracker

DATE DUE	EXPENSES	AMOUNT	PAID	DATE DUE	EXPENSES	AMOUNT	PAID

MONTH OF : _____
NOTES:

Goal	Achievement	Status

Monthly Planner and Expense Tracker

DATE DUE	EXPENSES	AMOUNT	PAID	DATE DUE	EXPENSES	AMOUNT	PAID

MONTH OF : _____
NOTES:

Goal	Achievement	Status

Monthly Planner and Expense Tracker

DATE DUE	EXPENSES	AMOUNT	PAID	DATE DUE	EXPENSES	AMOUNT	PAID

MONTH OF : _____
NOTES:

Goal	Achievement	Status

Monthly Planner and Expense Tracker

DATE DUE	EXPENSES	AMOUNT	PAID	DATE DUE	EXPENSES	AMOUNT	PAID

MONTH OF : _____
NOTES:

Goal	Achievement	Status

Monthly Planner and Expense Tracker

DATE DUE	EXPENSES	AMOUNT	PAID	DATE DUE	EXPENSES	AMOUNT	PAID

MONTH OF : _____
NOTES:

Goal	Achievement	Status

Monthly Planner and Expense Tracker

DATE DUE	EXPENSES	AMOUNT	PAID	DATE DUE	EXPENSES	AMOUNT	PAID

MONTH OF : _____
NOTES:

Goal	Achievement	Status

Monthly Planner and Expense Tracker

DATE DUE	EXPENSES	AMOUNT	PAID	DATE DUE	EXPENSES	AMOUNT	PAID

MONTH OF : _____
NOTES:

Goal	Achievement	Status

Monthly Planner and Expense Tracker

DATE DUE	EXPENSES	AMOUNT	PAID	DATE DUE	EXPENSES	AMOUNT	PAID

MONTH OF : _____
NOTES:

Goal	Achievement	Status

Monthly Planner and Expense Tracker

DATE DUE	EXPENSES	AMOUNT	PAID	DATE DUE	EXPENSES	AMOUNT	PAID

MONTH OF : _____
NOTES:

Goal	Achievement	Status

Monthly Planner and Expense Tracker

DATE DUE	EXPENSES	AMOUNT	PAID	DATE DUE	EXPENSES	AMOUNT	PAID

MONTH OF: _____
NOTES:

Goal	Achievement	Status

Monthly Planner and Expense Tracker

DATE DUE	EXPENSES	AMOUNT	PAID	DATE DUE	EXPENSES	AMOUNT	PAID

MONTH OF : _____
NOTES:

Goal	Achievement	Status

Monthly Planner and Expense Tracker

DATE DUE	EXPENSES	AMOUNT	PAID	DATE DUE	EXPENSES	AMOUNT	PAID

MONTH OF : _____
NOTES:

Goal	Achievement	Status

Monthly Planner and Expense Tracker

DATE DUE	EXPENSES	AMOUNT	PAID	DATE DUE	EXPENSES	AMOUNT	PAID

MONTH OF : _____
NOTES:

Goal	Achievement	Status

Monthly Planner and Expense Tracker

DATE DUE	EXPENSES	AMOUNT	PAID	DATE DUE	EXPENSES	AMOUNT	PAID

MONTH OF : _____
NOTES:

Goal	Achievement	Status

Monthly Planner and Expense Tracker

DATE DUE	EXPENSES	AMOUNT	PAID	DATE DUE	EXPENSES	AMOUNT	PAID

MONTH OF : _____
NOTES:

Goal	Achievement	Status

Monthly Planner and Expense Tracker

DATE DUE	EXPENSES	AMOUNT	PAID	DATE DUE	EXPENSES	AMOUNT	PAID

MONTH OF : _____
NOTES:

Goal	Achievement	Status

Monthly Planner and Expense Tracker

DATE DUE	EXPENSES	AMOUNT	PAID	DATE DUE	EXPENSES	AMOUNT	PAID

MONTH OF : _____
NOTES:

Goal	Achievement	Status

Monthly Planner and Expense Tracker

DATE DUE	EXPENSES	AMOUNT	PAID	DATE DUE	EXPENSES	AMOUNT	PAID

MONTH OF : _____
NOTES:

Goal	Achievement	Status

Monthly Planner and Expense Tracker

DATE DUE	EXPENSES	AMOUNT	PAID	DATE DUE	EXPENSES	AMOUNT	PAID

MONTH OF : _____
NOTES:

Goal	Achievement	Status

Monthly Planner and Expense Tracker

DATE DUE	EXPENSES	AMOUNT	PAID	DATE DUE	EXPENSES	AMOUNT	PAID

MONTH OF : _____
NOTES:

Goal	Achievement	Status

Monthly Planner and Expense Tracker

DATE DUE	EXPENSES	AMOUNT	PAID	DATE DUE	EXPENSES	AMOUNT	PAID

MONTH OF : _____
NOTES:

Goal	Achievement	Status

Monthly Planner and Expense Tracker

DATE DUE	EXPENSES	AMOUNT	PAID	DATE DUE	EXPENSES	AMOUNT	PAID

MONTH OF : _____
NOTES:

Goal	Achievement	Status

Monthly Planner and Expense Tracker

DATE DUE	EXPENSES	AMOUNT	PAID	DATE DUE	EXPENSES	AMOUNT	PAID

MONTH OF : _____
NOTES:

Goal	Achievement	Status

Monthly Planner and Expense Tracker

DATE DUE	EXPENSES	AMOUNT	PAID	DATE DUE	EXPENSES	AMOUNT	PAID

MONTH OF : _____
NOTES:

Goal	Achievement	Status

Monthly Planner and Expense Tracker

DATE DUE	EXPENSES	AMOUNT	PAID	DATE DUE	EXPENSES	AMOUNT	PAID

MONTH OF : _____
NOTES:

Goal	Achievement	Status

Monthly Planner and Expense Tracker

DATE DUE	EXPENSES	AMOUNT	PAID	DATE DUE	EXPENSES	AMOUNT	PAID

MONTH OF : _____
NOTES:

Goal	Achievement	Status

Monthly Planner and Expense Tracker

DATE DUE	EXPENSES	AMOUNT	PAID	DATE DUE	EXPENSES	AMOUNT	PAID

MONTH OF : _____
NOTES:

Goal	Achievement	Status

Monthly Planner and Expense Tracker

DATE DUE	EXPENSES	AMOUNT	PAID	DATE DUE	EXPENSES	AMOUNT	PAID

MONTH OF : _____
NOTES:

Goal	Achievement	Status

Monthly Planner and Expense Tracker

DATE DUE	EXPENSES	AMOUNT	PAID	DATE DUE	EXPENSES	AMOUNT	PAID

MONTH OF : _____
NOTES:

Goal	Achievement	Status

Monthly Planner and Expense Tracker

DATE DUE	EXPENSES	AMOUNT	PAID	DATE DUE	EXPENSES	AMOUNT	PAID

MONTH OF : _____
NOTES:

Goal	Achievement	Status

Monthly Planner and Expense Tracker

DATE DUE	EXPENSES	AMOUNT	PAID	DATE DUE	EXPENSES	AMOUNT	PAID

MONTH OF : _____
NOTES:

Goal	Achievement	Status

Monthly Planner and Expense Tracker

DATE DUE	EXPENSES	AMOUNT	PAID	DATE DUE	EXPENSES	AMOUNT	PAID

MONTH OF : _____
NOTES:

Goal	Achievement	Status

Monthly Planner and Expense Tracker

DATE DUE	EXPENSES	AMOUNT	PAID	DATE DUE	EXPENSES	AMOUNT	PAID

MONTH OF : _____
NOTES:

Goal	Achievement	Status

Monthly Planner and Expense Tracker

DATE DUE	EXPENSES	AMOUNT	PAID	DATE DUE	EXPENSES	AMOUNT	PAID

MONTH OF : _____
NOTES:

Goal	Achievement	Status

Monthly Planner and Expense Tracker

DATE DUE	EXPENSES	AMOUNT	PAID	DATE DUE	EXPENSES	AMOUNT	PAID

MONTH OF : _____
NOTES:

Goal	Achievement	Status

Monthly Planner and Expense Tracker

DATE DUE	EXPENSES	AMOUNT	PAID	DATE DUE	EXPENSES	AMOUNT	PAID

MONTH OF : _____
NOTES:

Goal	Achievement	Status

Monthly Planner and Expense Tracker

DATE DUE	EXPENSES	AMOUNT	PAID	DATE DUE	EXPENSES	AMOUNT	PAID

MONTH OF : _____
NOTES:

Goal	Achievement	Status

Monthly Planner and Expense Tracker

DATE DUE	EXPENSES	AMOUNT	PAID	DATE DUE	EXPENSES	AMOUNT	PAID

MONTH OF : _____
NOTES:

Goal	Achievement	Status

Monthly Planner and Expense Tracker

DATE DUE	EXPENSES	AMOUNT	PAID	DATE DUE	EXPENSES	AMOUNT	PAID

MONTH OF : _____
NOTES:

Goal	Achievement	Status

Monthly Planner and Expense Tracker

DATE DUE	EXPENSES	AMOUNT	PAID	DATE DUE	EXPENSES	AMOUNT	PAID

MONTH OF : _____
NOTES:

Goal	Achievement	Status

Monthly Planner and Expense Tracker

DATE DUE	EXPENSES	AMOUNT	PAID	DATE DUE	EXPENSES	AMOUNT	PAID

MONTH OF : _____
NOTES:

Goal	Achievement	Status

Monthly Planner and Expense Tracker

DATE DUE	EXPENSES	AMOUNT	PAID	DATE DUE	EXPENSES	AMOUNT	PAID

MONTH OF : _____
NOTES:

Goal	Achievement	Status

Monthly Planner and Expense Tracker

DATE DUE	EXPENSES	AMOUNT	PAID	DATE DUE	EXPENSES	AMOUNT	PAID

MONTH OF : _____
NOTES:

Goal	Achievement	Status

Monthly Planner and Expense Tracker

DATE DUE	EXPENSES	AMOUNT	PAID	DATE DUE	EXPENSES	AMOUNT	PAID

MONTH OF : _____
NOTES:

Goal	Achievement	Status

Monthly Planner and Expense Tracker

DATE DUE	EXPENSES	AMOUNT	PAID	DATE DUE	EXPENSES	AMOUNT	PAID

MONTH OF : _____
NOTES:

Goal	Achievement	Status

Monthly Planner and Expense Tracker

DATE DUE	EXPENSES	AMOUNT	PAID	DATE DUE	EXPENSES	AMOUNT	PAID

MONTH OF : _____
NOTES:

Goal	Achievement	Status

Monthly Planner and Expense Tracker

DATE DUE	EXPENSES	AMOUNT	PAID	DATE DUE	EXPENSES	AMOUNT	PAID

MONTH OF : _____
NOTES:

Goal	Achievement	Status

Monthly Planner and Expense Tracker

DATE DUE	EXPENSES	AMOUNT	PAID	DATE DUE	EXPENSES	AMOUNT	PAID

MONTH OF : _____
NOTES:

Goal	Achievement	Status

Monthly Planner and Expense Tracker

DATE DUE	EXPENSES	AMOUNT	PAID	DATE DUE	EXPENSES	AMOUNT	PAID

MONTH OF : _____
NOTES:

Goal	Achievement	Status

Monthly Planner and Expense Tracker

DATE DUE	EXPENSES	AMOUNT	PAID	DATE DUE	EXPENSES	AMOUNT	PAID

MONTH OF : _____
NOTES:

Goal	Achievement	Status

Monthly Planner and Expense Tracker

DATE DUE	EXPENSES	AMOUNT	PAID	DATE DUE	EXPENSES	AMOUNT	PAID

MONTH OF : _____
NOTES:

Goal	Achievement	Status

Monthly Planner and Expense Tracker

DATE DUE	EXPENSES	AMOUNT	PAID	DATE DUE	EXPENSES	AMOUNT	PAID

MONTH OF : _____
NOTES:

Goal	Achievement	Status

Monthly Planner and Expense Tracker

DATE DUE	EXPENSES	AMOUNT	PAID	DATE DUE	EXPENSES	AMOUNT	PAID

MONTH OF : _____
NOTES:

Goal	Achievement	Status

Monthly Planner and Expense Tracker

DATE DUE	EXPENSES	AMOUNT	PAID	DATE DUE	EXPENSES	AMOUNT	PAID

MONTH OF : _____
NOTES:

Goal	Achievement	Status

Monthly Planner and Expense Tracker

DATE DUE	EXPENSES	AMOUNT	PAID	DATE DUE	EXPENSES	AMOUNT	PAID

MONTH OF : _____
NOTES:

Goal	Achievement	Status

Monthly Planner and Expense Tracker

DATE DUE	EXPENSES	AMOUNT	PAID	DATE DUE	EXPENSES	AMOUNT	PAID

MONTH OF : _____
NOTES:

Goal	Achievement	Status

Monthly Planner and Expense Tracker

DATE DUE	EXPENSES	AMOUNT	PAID	DATE DUE	EXPENSES	AMOUNT	PAID

MONTH OF : _____
NOTES:

Goal	Achievement	Status

Monthly Planner and Expense Tracker

DATE DUE	EXPENSES	AMOUNT	PAID	DATE DUE	EXPENSES	AMOUNT	PAID

MONTH OF : _____
NOTES:

Goal	Achievement	Status

Monthly Planner and Expense Tracker

DATE DUE	EXPENSES	AMOUNT	PAID	DATE DUE	EXPENSES	AMOUNT	PAID

MONTH OF : _____
NOTES:

Goal	Achievement	Status

Monthly Planner and Expense Tracker

DATE DUE	EXPENSES	AMOUNT	PAID	DATE DUE	EXPENSES	AMOUNT	PAID

MONTH OF : _____
NOTES:

Goal	Achievement	Status

Monthly Planner and Expense Tracker

DATE DUE	EXPENSES	AMOUNT	PAID	DATE DUE	EXPENSES	AMOUNT	PAID

MONTH OF : _____
NOTES:

Goal	Achievement	Status

Monthly Planner and Expense Tracker

DATE DUE	EXPENSES	AMOUNT	PAID	DATE DUE	EXPENSES	AMOUNT	PAID

MONTH OF : _____
NOTES:

Goal	Achievement	Status

Monthly Planner and Expense Tracker

DATE DUE	EXPENSES	AMOUNT	PAID	DATE DUE	EXPENSES	AMOUNT	PAID

MONTH OF : _____
NOTES:

Goal	Achievement	Status

Monthly Planner and Expense Tracker

DATE DUE	EXPENSES	AMOUNT	PAID	DATE DUE	EXPENSES	AMOUNT	PAID

MONTH OF : _____
NOTES:

Goal	Achievement	Status

Monthly Planner and Expense Tracker

DATE DUE	EXPENSES	AMOUNT	PAID	DATE DUE	EXPENSES	AMOUNT	PAID

MONTH OF : _____
NOTES:

Goal	Achievement	Status

Monthly Planner and Expense Tracker

DATE DUE	EXPENSES	AMOUNT	PAID	DATE DUE	EXPENSES	AMOUNT	PAID

MONTH OF : _____
NOTES:

Goal	Achievement	Status

Monthly Planner and Expense Tracker

DATE DUE	EXPENSES	AMOUNT	PAID	DATE DUE	EXPENSES	AMOUNT	PAID

MONTH OF : _____
NOTES:

Goal	Achievement	Status

Monthly Planner and Expense Tracker

DATE DUE	EXPENSES	AMOUNT	PAID	DATE DUE	EXPENSES	AMOUNT	PAID

MONTH OF : _____
NOTES:

Goal	Achievement	Status

Monthly Planner and Expense Tracker

DATE DUE	EXPENSES	AMOUNT	PAID	DATE DUE	EXPENSES	AMOUNT	PAID

MONTH OF : _____
NOTES:

Goal	Achievement	Status

www.ingramcontent.com/pod-product-compliance
Lightning Source LLC
Chambersburg PA
CBHW081438220526
45466CB00008B/2433